The farm in spring

Jenny Giles
Illustrated by Isabel Lowe

We can see
a gray horse
with one foal.

We can see

a brown cow

with two calves.

We can see

a white sheep

with three lambs.

We can see
a black dog
with four puppies.

We can see
an orange cat
with five kittens.

We can see
a pink pig
with six piglets.

13

We can see

a red hen

with seven chicks.

We can see

1, 2, 3, 4, 5, 6, 7, 8

little yellow ducklings.